THE WAY OF THE CROSS WITH ST. JOHN THE APOSTLE

By

Monsignor Eric R. Barr, S.T.L.

Illustrations by Sister Mary Grace Thul, O.P.

THE WAY OF THE CROSS WITH ST. JOHN THE APOSTLE

Cover art and interior art by Sister Mary Grace Thul, O.P.

Published courtesy of Telemachus Press, LLC
7652 Sawmill Road
Suite 304
Dublin, Ohio 43016
http://www.telemachuspress.com

Visit the author website:
www.erbarr.com

First published in the August 1992
issue of *THE PRIEST MAGAZINE.*

ISBN: 978-1-948046-43-5 (eBook)
ISBN: 978-1-948046-44-2 (Paperback)

Library of Congress Control Number: 2019931482

Version 2019.01.29

First published in the August 1992 issue of *The Priest Magazine*, *The Way of the Cross with St. John the Apostle* has been used since throughout the Diocese of Rockford, Illinois.

This book is prayerfully dedicated to the priests of the Diocese of Rockford who walk the Way of the Cross in their daily lives, ministering to
the People of God.

PRAYING THE WAY OF THE CROSS

The Way Of The Cross, also known as The Stations Of The Cross, is both a public and private devotion meditating on fourteen events of the last day of the life of Christ. These stations or events are drawn from both Scripture and Tradition.

Pilgrimage to Jerusalem to pray at the various locations where Christ's Passion and Death occurred began by 325 A.D. after St. Helena discovered the relics of the True Cross, and her son, the Emperor Constantine, built the Church of the Holy Sepulcher over the burial tomb of Jesus. The Stations, as we know them now, began to take shape in the fourteenth century when the Franciscans took charge of the Holy Sites in Jerusalem. Most Christians could not make the pilgrimage to the Holy Land, and gradually, Stations were set up inside churches to pray the Way Of The Cross. Pope Clement XII in 1731 set the number of Stations at fourteen, and by the middle of the nineteenth century, most Catholic Churches had a set of Stations, usually pictures or sculptures of Christ's Passion and Death on the interior walls of the Church. The Way Of The Cross is exceedingly popular today especially during the liturgical season of Lent.

There are many different varieties of the Stations of the Cross focusing on different aspects of the sufferings of Jesus. The purpose of all of them is to help a person prayerfully reflect on how Jesus's suffering and death redeemed people and how the Passion of Christ affects our lives today. This particular version—THE WAY OF THE CROSS WITH ST. JOHN THE APOSTLE—looks on these events from the perspective of the youngest of the apostles and the best friend of Jesus.

Praying these Stations is self-evident and may be done in private or with a group, at home or in a church. If in a church, a person may walk from Station to Station as the prayer progresses.

The words of St. Francis of Assisi are used at the beginning of each Station: "We adore you O Christ, and we praise you; because by your Holy Cross you have redeemed the world." As those words are prayed, one genuflects or bows.

At the end of each Station the words, "Jesus, remember me when you come into your Kingdom," are said or sung twice. If sung, the Taize version is preferred as most churches have the music.

If a priest or deacon is leading the Way of the Cross, it may conclude with the Benediction of the Blessed Sacrament.

THE WAY OF THE CROSS WITH ST. JOHN THE APOSTLE

INTRODUCTION

Opening Hymn

Leader: My name is John, apostle of the Lord Jesus. Thank you for being here today on this dusty street in Jerusalem. All the other apostles have fled in fear for their lives, and I am in need of companions on this terrible journey. The mother of Jesus and I need you. We cannot walk this way alone, this way of death which Jesus takes—alone. Mary and I walk with him, but we cannot die for him. No, he dies for us, and for the world. All we can do is weep. Mary weeps for the son she raised, I for the best and dearest friend I have ever had. Jesus Christ is going to die on the hill of Calvary. Will you walk with us—with the mother of Jesus and me? For though we cannot save him, if we walk by his side and stand at the foot of the Cross, he will know we love him and will follow him always. Will you walk with us?

People: **We will walk with you.**
We will walk the way of Calvary,
with Mary and with John.
We will follow Christ and share his suffering,
his pain, his death upon a tree.

Leader: The Light shines in the darkness.

People: **Death shall have no victory.**

People: **Jesus, remember me, when you come into your kingdom.**
Jesus, remember me, when you come into your kingdom.

THE FIRST STATION
JESUS IS CONDEMNED TO DEATH

Leader: We adore you O Christ and we praise you.
    (genuflect as this is said)

People: **Because by your Holy Cross,
you have redeemed the world.**

Leader: This morning, Pilate sentenced Jesus to death. The crowds demanded it, and Pilate, wishing to please Caesar, gave in to the mob in the street and condemned Christ. Caught in the middle of the screaming rabble, I heard them shout for Christ's death, cry for his blood. Those who loved him and honored him with palms when he entered Jerusalem now thirsted for his destruction. With Judas they betrayed the Lord. Why? All he had given them was love and healing and hope. Why did they forsake him?

People: **We all betray Jesus, whenever we ridicule a friend, mock a neighbor, insult the stranger. We all betray him, for the same reason as Judas and the mob:**
- **Afraid to stand alone, we lose ourselves in the crowd.**
- **Afraid to stand alone, we let others determine right and wrong for us.**
- **Afraid to stand alone, we turn our backs on Christ, because we are afraid.**

In sorrow we grieve, from our fear we shall be free.

Leader: The Light shines in the darkness.

People: **Death shall have no victory.**

People: **Jesus, remember me, when you come into your kingdom.
Jesus, remember me, when you come into your kingdom.**

THE SECOND STATION
JESUS IS MADE TO CARRY HIS CROSS

Leader: We adore you O Christ and we praise you.

**People: Because by your Holy Cross,
you have redeemed the world.**

Leader: Look at the heavy cross beam placed on the neck and shoulders of my Lord. They tie his arms, his face twists in pain, but he accepts the wood and turns not his head. If only I could carry it for you Lord, if only I could bear your cross.

People: We see the cross and feel the pain. It is a familiar burden. Though we have never carried such a terrible weight, yet portions of this cross also lay across our shoulders:

- **the burden of sins**
- **the heaviness of sorrows**
- **the weight of sickness.**

We accept our burdens, these pieces of the cross we carry, and know they are carried first by our Lord. If he can bear our sins and pain, surely, we can walk with him to Calvary.

Leader: The Light shines in the darkness.

People: Death shall have no victory.

**People: Jesus, remember me, when you come into your kingdom.
Jesus, remember me, when you come into your kingdom.**

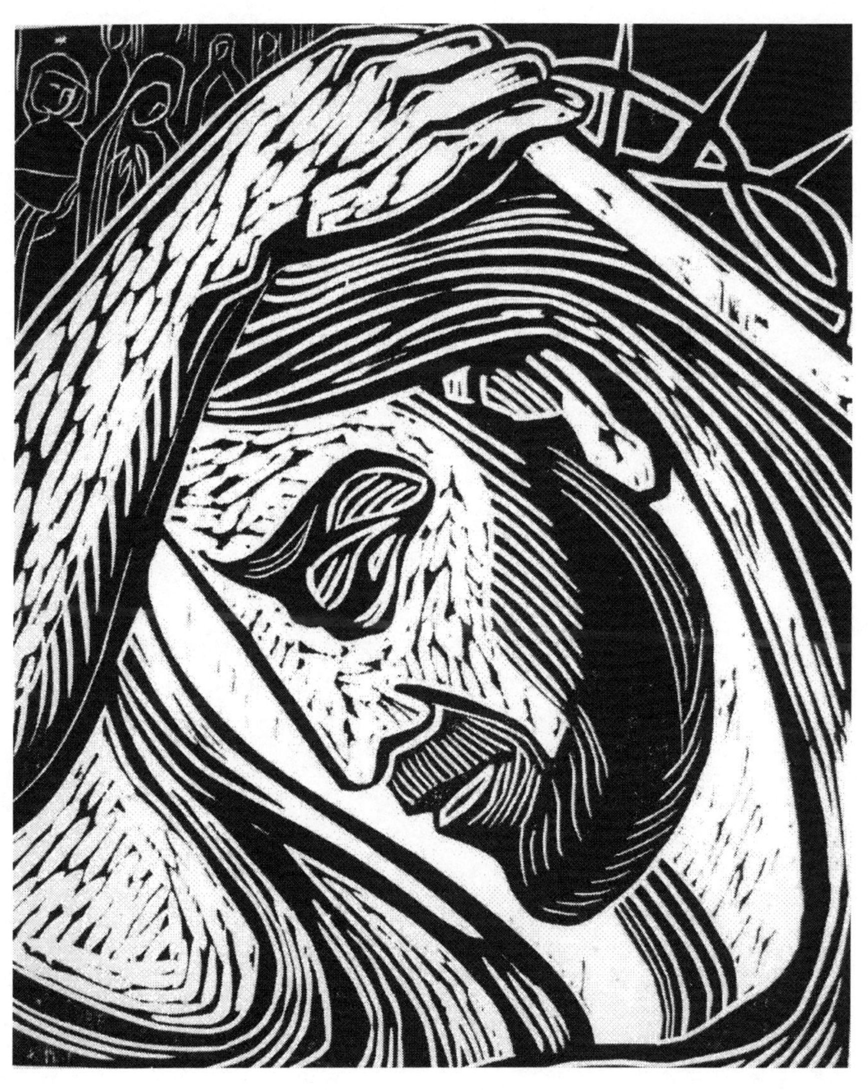

THE THIRD STATION
Jesus Falls The First Time

Leader: We adore you O Christ and we praise you.

People: **Because by your Holy Cross,
you have redeemed the world.**

Leader: Under the weight of the wood, he falls on the sharp cobblestones of the street. But even before the soldiers start whipping him, he tries to get up. He asked me once, "John, can you drink from the cup I drink?" I thought I could then, but now, my Lord bleeds from countless wounds. If I carried the cross and fell, would I have the strength to rise again?

People: **Christ collapses, yet struggles on. How often have we fallen and failed to rise, willing to let our weakness conquer us, willing to let sin defeat us, willing to let our pain overcome us? With John and Mary we see him stand again. Pain-ravaged face but eyes clear and strong, one glance at us as if to say, "Stay close to me and find the strength to carry on; stay close, my friends, to me."**

Leader: The Light shines in the darkness.

People: **Death shall have no victory.**

People: **Jesus, remember me, when you come into your kingdom.
Jesus, remember me, when you come into your kingdom.**

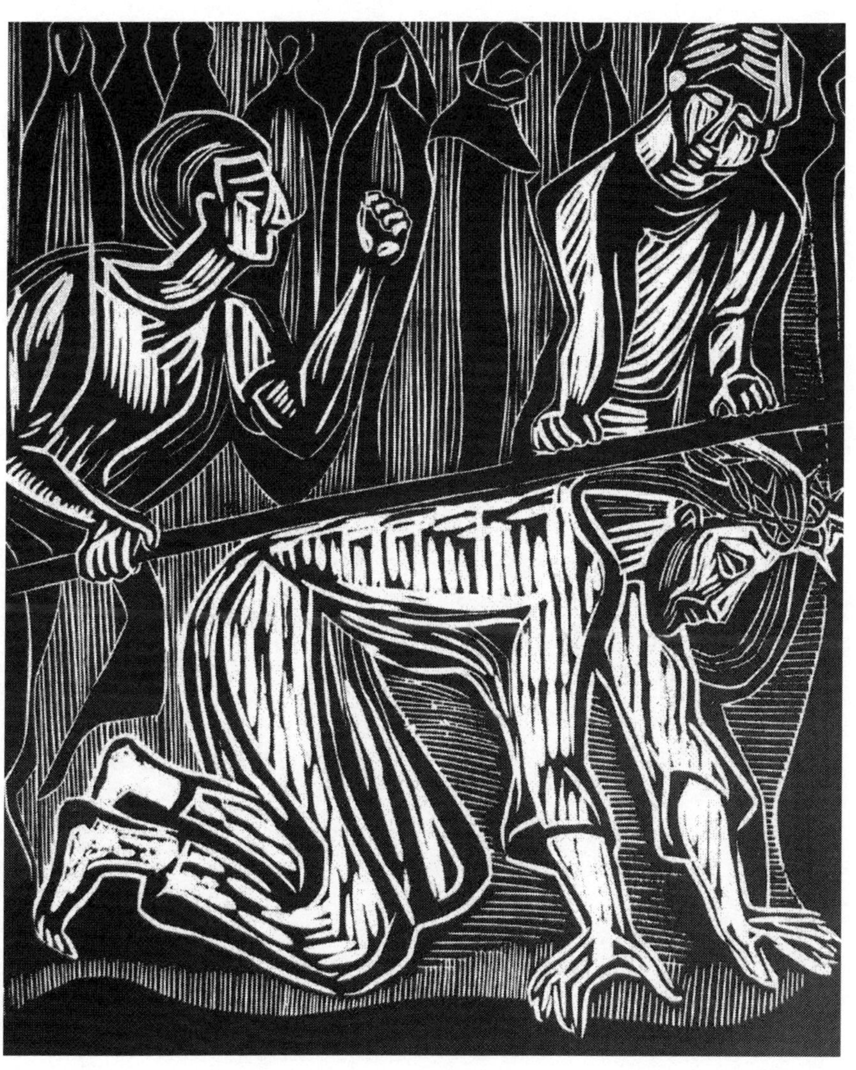

THE FOURTH STATION
Jesus Meets His Mother

Leader: We adore you O Christ and we praise you.

People: **Because by your Holy Cross,
you have redeemed the world.**

Leader: Mary breaks away from me, and pushes her way through the crowd and soldiers to tend her wounded son. Gently she touches the blood-spattered, sweat drenched face of my Lord. And gently, he smiles at her loving act of kindness. Only a moment and the soldiers push her away. I cannot ease her pain. As she weeps for her son, she carries his agony in her heart.

People: **O Mary, a sword of sorrow has pierced you through. As you watch your only son walk slowly toward his death, how great your grief, how terrible your sadness! Jesus carries the weight of the world's anguish on his back. O Mother of Sorrows weep for us as well:**

- **we who have broken families**
- **we who have sick parents**
- **we who have lost a loved one through death**
- **we who suffer from shattered relationships.**

Let your faithfulness give us courage; may your strength help us see.

Leader: The Light shines in the darkness.

People: **Death shall have no victory.**

People: **Jesus, remember me, when you come into your kingdom.
Jesus, remember me, when you come into your kingdom.**

THE FIFTH STATION
Simon Of Cyrene Helps Jesus Carry His Cross

Leader: We adore you O Christ and we praise you.

**People: Because by your Holy Cross,
you have redeemed the world.**

Leader: No matter how hard they beat my Lord, he is too weak to go on without help. The soldiers reach into the crowd and grab a man to help Jesus. The stranger's face is full of fear, as if just by being near Jesus he will be accused of being his accomplice. Yet, as he looks at the face of Christ, his fear vanishes and willingly he helps shoulder the burden, so that my Lord may continue on.

People: We know Simon's fear. In school, at the workplace, among friends the questions are asked:
- **Why do you believe?**
- **Do you really think Christ is the answer?**
- **Are you going to follow your faith or do what everyone else is doing?**
- **Make a choice!**

Risking ridicule, loss of friends and even our job, we must walk forward and let the crowd and soldiers see. Despite our fear we will help carry the cross willingly.

Leader: The Light shines in the darkness.

People: Death shall have no victory.

**People: Jesus, remember me, when you come into your kingdom.
Jesus, remember me, when you come into your kingdom.**

THE SIXTH STATION
VERONICA WIPES THE FACE OF JESUS

Leader: We adore you O Christ and we praise you.

People: **Because by your Holy Cross,
you have redeemed the world.**

Leader: Not all the crowd is hostile to my Lord. A woman steps forward and stops Jesus. Strangely, the soldiers allow her to wipe the blood and sweat off the face of my Lord. Again no words, just a look of gratefulness from Jesus, and he moves on toward the hill where his crucifixion waits. But the woman gasps in awe at the cloth she used, for instead of blood and sweat the face of my Lord is imprinted on the cloth.

People: **So many times we have looked into the faces of the suffering:**
- **the homeless**
- **the hungry**
- **the unemployed**
- **the sick.**

Often, we have simply walked away. But the times we have stopped, like Veronica, to ease their suffering, we have seen what she saw—the face of Christ looking back at us. Often walks the Christ in the stranger's clothes. Lord, give us the compassion of Veronica and make us know that any time someone looks at us with eyes of suffering, it is your face we see.

Leader: The Light shines in the darkness.

People: **Death shall have no victory.**

People: **Jesus, remember me, when you come into your kingdom.
Jesus, remember me, when you come into your kingdom.**

THE SEVENTH STATION
Jesus Falls The Second Time

Leader: We adore you O Christ and we praise you.

**People: Because by your Holy Cross,
you have redeemed the world.**

Leader: I watch him fall again. My God, how can you let this happen to your servant, to your Son? The soldiers jerk him roughly to his feet and beat him onward. I do not think he will have the strength to go much farther. Just before my friends fled last night, they told me they could not understand how one so blessed could be so abandoned by God. I must confess the same question haunts me.

People: Confusion—we share it with you and the other apostles. Christ is not the only one we have watched die an unjust death. We have seen:
- **the aged wasting away in nursing homes**
- **the child stricken with terminal illness**
- **good people touched by tragedies not of their making.**

And we, too, ask, *"Why?"* And we receive no answer but what we see here. Our Lord gets up and trudges onward. Only he seems confident that God is still with him. What secret does he know; what hope does he hold on to so fiercely?

Leader: The Light shines in the darkness.

People: Death shall have no victory.

**People: Jesus, remember me, when you come into your kingdom.
Jesus, remember me, when you come into your kingdom.**

THE EIGHTH STATION
JESUS MEETS THE WOMEN OF JERUSALEM

Leader: We adore you O Christ and we praise you.

**People: Because by your Holy Cross,
you have redeemed the world.**

Leader: Several women now break out from the crowd and fall at the feet of Jesus, weeping. Before he is forced to pass them by, he speaks to them, telling them not to weep for him but for themselves and for their children. For if those who hate the Light do not recognize who Christ is and kill him, what will those enemies do to other innocents when he is gone?

People: Lord, your warning strikes a chord of truth in our lives, for we live in a world that does not honor you nor the values you stood for, a world of

- **wars and terrorism**
- **indiscriminate violence and random murder**
- **lying and cheating on small and massive scales**
- **drug and alcohol addictions.**

These are only some of the sins afflicting us, and yes, we weep for they cause us great pain. Deliver us from these horrors, save us from these agonies.

Leader: The Light shines in the darkness.

People: Death shall have no victory.

**People: Jesus, remember me, when you come into your kingdom.
Jesus, remember me, when you come into your kingdom.**

THE NINTH STATION
Jesus Falls The Third Time

Leader: We adore you O Christ and we praise you.

People: **Because by your Holy Cross,
you have redeemed the world.**

Leader: At the foot of Calvary, my Lord falls a third time. His burden is nearly too great for him. He cannot move and the soldiers have to lift him up upon his feet and send him stumbling the short distance to the place of crucifixion. How different he looks now than when Peter, James and I saw him transfigured in glory on the mountain. He said he had come to give his life as a ransom for the many. Is this the price of glory?

People: **Jesus, what you have undergone to save us! Only now, after this third fall, can we feel the pain you must have suffered. Yet you never give up, so conscious of your Father's will and the destiny you have been given. Christ, scorned and rejected;**
- **keep us from being overcome by our sins**
- **save us from the misfortunes that befall us**
- **give us courage to walk beside you despite our weaknesses, despite our fears.**

Leader: The Light shines in the darkness.

People: **Death shall have no victory.**

People: **Jesus, remember me, when you come into your kingdom.
Jesus, remember me, when you come into your kingdom.**

THE TENTH STATION
JESUS IS STRIPPED OF HIS GARMENTS

Leader: We adore you O Christ and we praise you.

**People: Because by your Holy Cross,
you have redeemed the world.**

Leader: They rip the crossbeam off the shoulders of my Lord, and now they strip him of his garments. His back bleeds anew where they scourged him. Bruises cover his body. He stands before the crowd, stripped of his dignity. The body that was touched reverently by those he healed and those who welcomed him into Jerusalem with palms of honor, now that body is spit upon, and struck again. Lord, my friend, what have they done to you?

People: Jesus, when we think of the indignity you endured, how can we not help but think of the ways we strip ourselves of our own dignity by abusing our own or other's bodies through violence, misplaced sexuality, drugs or alcohol. When we deliberately strip ourselves or others of human worth, we are in league with your torturers; when others abuse us, we stand with you at Calvary, victims of humanity's inhumanity. For those who have suffered as you have suffered, Lord, give them dignity.

Leader: The Light shines in the darkness.

People: Death shall have no victory.

**People: Jesus, remember me, when you come into your kingdom.
Jesus, remember me, when you come into your kingdom.**

THE ELEVENTH STATION
JESUS IS NAILED TO THE CROSS

Leader: We adore you O Christ and we praise you.

**People: Because by your Holy Cross,
you have redeemed the world.**

Leader: The mother of Christ buries her face on my shoulder as the first nail is hammered into the hand of her son. She cannot bear to look, but I must as I see the violence done to my Lord. The bones are wrenched and the muscles are stretched so that the suffering will be most intense. And though he is exhausted from his ordeal, no cries of agony escape his lips as the nails pierce and the soldiers raise him up on the cross, there to bleed, there to die.

People: It is hard to go forward and see the pain of Mary, the terror of John, the horrible suffering of Christ. How do you endure, Lord? Is your love so great that you can suffer so terribly? Without your help, how can we ever survive our own crosses? Teach us, Lord, to use our pain as a prayer for others
- **to endure our suffering in imitation of you**
- **to accept whatever may happen in our lives as you accepted your cross: joyfully, courageously, faithfully.**

Leader: The Light shines in the darkness.

People: Death shall have no victory.

**People: Jesus, remember me, when you come into your kingdom.
Jesus, remember me, when you come into your kingdom.**

THE TWELFTH STATION
JESUS DIES ON THE CROSS

Leader: We adore you O Christ and we praise you.

**People: Because by your Holy Cross,
you have redeemed the world.**

Leader: As my Lord hangs in agony, the mother of Jesus and I walk to the foot of the cross. I put aside my fear for Mary needs to be near her son. And so we stand and look up in grief as the hope of the world dies. He looks down at Mary and says to his mother, "Woman behold your son," glancing at me. Then, with eyes of infinite compassion upon me, he says, "Behold your mother." And he gives her into my care. I see him raise his head and look at you, my friends. Can you see his eyes? Do you hear him speak? What does he say to you?

All kneel briefly in silent meditation.

People: O Lord, as Blessed Mary and John look up at you, you breathe your last. "It is finished," you say. Out of love for us, you have died. You have died to save us from our sins. From our sins you have set us free, hanging there upon the tree, upon the tree at Calvary.

Leader: The Light shines in the darkness.

People: Death shall have no victory.

**People: Jesus, remember me, when you come into your kingdom.
Jesus, remember me, when you come into your kingdom.**

THE THIRTEENTH STATION
Jesus Is Taken Down From His Cross

Leader: We adore you O Christ and we praise you.

People: **Because by your Holy Cross,
you have redeemed the world.**

Leader: Into the arms of his mother, I give the body of Jesus. No grief has ever been so great as that moment when Mary holds the body of her crucified Son. Christ ends his earthly life as he began it, next to the heart of his mother. O Mary, if only I could ease your pain, I the least of his followers. But I could not stop his death, how can I still your sorrow?

People: **Under the shadow of the cross, she grieves and we with her. The sun is darkened, tremors fill the earth as all creation groans in agony over the death of the Son of God. O Lord, your death has wounded us deeply, reminding us of**

- **the death of parents and children**
- **the loss of friends and neighbors**
- **even the death of our hopes and dreams.**

We stand stunned in sorrow over the powers that yet loom in this world to snatch life away, and in the darkness at the foot of the cross, we grieve with Mary as she cries, "Who will give me back my son, who will give my son back to me?"

Leader: The Light shines in the darkness.

People: **Death shall have no victory.**

People: **Jesus, remember me, when you come into your kingdom.
Jesus, remember me, when you come into your kingdom.**

THE FOURTEENTH STATION
JESUS IS LAID IN THE TOMB

Leader: We adore you O Christ and we praise you.

**People: Because by your Holy Cross,
you have redeemed the world.**

Leader: A wealthy man, Joseph of Arimathea has given a stone tomb for the burial of Jesus. A gift of generosity from a man who greatly admired my Lord. But we must hurry now, for the Sabbath is nearly here. We wrap the body of Jesus in a shroud and lay him in the tomb. I and others roll the stone across the entrance. As evening falls, Mary and I stand in silence in this place of rest. Is it truly over? I wonder.

People: O Lord, after such a passion and death, you rest now in your tomb. Death has taken you as it takes us all. But can the one who raised Jairus' daughter, or snatched the widow's son back from the jaws of death, or brought Lazarus back to life—can such a one truly stay dead? Lord drive away our doubts. So often you said,
- **"I am the Light of the world."**
- **"I am the Bread of Life."**
- **"I am the Resurrection and the Life."**

Break the chains of death so that we can live, so that we can believe, so that we can see.

Leader: The Light shines in the darkness.

People: Death shall have no victory.

**People: Jesus, remember me, when you come into your kingdom.
Jesus, remember me, when you come into your kingdom.**

CONCLUSION

Leader: I know now the truth of the Cross.
I see it in your faces,
You who have walked with me.
The cross is not an end,
For he said he would rise.
The tomb is not an end,
But rather the beginning.

People: **In the beginning was the Word,**
And the Word was with God,
And the Word was God.
He was in the beginning with God.
All things came to be through him,
And without him nothing came to be.
What came to be through him was life.
And this life was the light of the human race;
The light shines in the darkness,
And the darkness has not overcome it...
The Word became flesh
And made his dwelling among us,
And we saw his glory,
The glory as of the Father's only Son,
Full of grace and truth.

John 1:1-5, 14

Closing Hymn

Made in the USA
Monee, IL
07 July 2026